CLY*

LEGENDS
OF THE WEST

The Black Cowboys

Butch Cassidy

Wyatt Earp

The Gunslingers

Jesse James

Annie Oakley

LEGENDS OF THE WEST

THE BLACK COWBOYS

John Wukovits

CHELSEA HOUSE PUBLISHERS

Philadelphia

CHELSEA HOUSE PUBLISHERS
Editor-in-Chief : Stephen Reginald
Managing Editor : James D. Gallagher
Production Manager : Pamela Loos
Art Director : Sara Davis
Picture Editor : Judy Hasday
Senior Production Editor : Lisa Chippendale

Staff for **THE BLACK COWBOYS**
Cover Design and Digital Illustration : Robert Gerson
Cover Photo Credit : Corbis-Bettmann
Picture Researcher : John F. Wukovits
Text Design : William Emerson, Jr.

First Printing

1 3 5 7 9 8 6 4 2

Library of Congress Cataloging-in-Publication Data

Wukovits, John F., 1944-
    The black cowboys / John Wukovits.
    p. cm. -- (Legends of the West)
Includes bibliographical references (p.) and index.
Summary: A history of the exploits of Jim Beckwourth, Bill
Pickett, Bose Ikard, and other Afro-American cowboys who
contributed to the development of the American West.
ISBN 0-7910-3907-2
1. Afro-American cowboys—West (U.S.)—History—Juvenile literature. 2. Afro-American cowboys—West (U.S.)—Biography—Juvenile literature. 3. West (U.S.)—History—Juvenile literature. 4. West (U.S.)—Biography—Juvenile literature. 5. Frontier and pioneer life—West (U.S)—Juvenile literature. [1. Afro-American cowboys—(West (U.S.) 2. West (U.S.)—History. 3. West (U.S.)—Biography. 4. Frontier and pioneer life—West (U.S)] I. Title. II. Series: Wukovits, John F., 1944- Legends of the West.
F596.W85 1997
978'. 00496073--dc21   97-2620
                                                        CIP
                                                        AC

CONTENTS

★

"I Wonder Why I Was Never Free Before"

During the 1800s, thousands of Americans abandoned homes scattered throughout the eastern half of the nation in hopes of finding a better life in the vast West. Some were lured by the prospects of adventure in the dangerous lands, where unfamiliar territory, wild beasts, and strange tribes of Indians combined to form perils not often encountered in the more settled parts of the United States. Profits from the fur trade or gold mining attracted large numbers, while others gathered their few belongings and trekked west because they wanted a better life than the one they had.

African Americans joined the steady stream west for the same reasons as anyone else, but

---

Like others of their countrymen, African Americans filled a variety of roles in the Wild West. In this picture, black police officers in the Indian Territory (Oklahoma) pose with their white counterparts.

because many had either been slaves or had come from a family whose African ancestors first arrived on the continent shackled in chains, the West meant more.

"This is free ground," exclaimed former slave John Lewis Solomon in 1879 when he, his wife, and their four children finally reached Kansas. "Then I looked on the heavens, and I said, 'That is free and beautiful heaven.' Then I looked within my heart, and I said to myself, 'I wonder why I was never free before.'"

Though African Americans in the West may have settled far from the region where slavery reigned, they never escaped the biting sting of prejudice. In some ways, especially as cowboys driving herds of cattle along the dusty trails where skill mattered more than color, blacks received a small measure of respect from their white cohorts, but they were never fully accepted. More outcasts than brethren, blacks in the West still occupied a second-class status.

Despite these difficulties, blacks streamed westward in ever-increasing numbers and produced some of the most stirring stories to grace the pages of American history. While, as with other groups who gazed longingly across the Mississippi River toward the opportunities offered by the endless prairies and majestic mountains, a small number employed their talents in less than honorable manners, unique individuals abounded whose courage, skill, and vision helped build a nation from a wilderness.

James Beckwourth was one such person. Born a slave on a Fredericksburg, Virginia plantation on April 26, 1798, Beckwourth arrived in the West in 1810 when his white master relocated near St. Louis, Missouri. Restless in spirit and uncomfortable among large numbers of people, he escaped not long after and drifted about the frontier, where he found solace in the isolation and independence offered by the dense forests and soaring mountains.

In 1823 Beckwourth joined the Rocky Mountain Fur Company. As a trapper of fur-bearing animals, he continued to work largely by himself, but he also knew that he could count on receiving money whenever he came down from the mountains with a bundle of fur for the trading post.

At six feet tall, sporting arms that bulged with muscles, Beckwourth presented an impressive sight. Bedecked with the gold chains he always wore around his neck, Beckwourth either braided his long hair or tied it back with colorful ribbons, and he pierced both ears in numerous places so that he could wear his many earrings. Beckwourth moved more quickly through forests or up mountain trails than other trappers, and few could defeat him in wrestling matches.

Beckwourth loved the wilderness, for there a man truly was treated as an equal. Nature unfolded its breathtaking beauty to anyone who proved tough enough to brave her hazards, while wild animals either shied away from any human who came too close, or they attacked without discrimination. Few people bothered Beckwourth in the mountains. If he succeeded, it would be because he had what it took to succeed. If he failed, he had no one to blame but himself.

Beckwourth survived many adventures in the wilderness. One winter, a wounded buffalo charged and almost killed the huge trapper. A group of Kansas Indians eventually found the weary Beckwourth, practically dead from star-

A man of incredible strength and courage, James Beckwourth lived with and fought against Native Americans, hunted wild animals in the Rocky Mountains, and helped open the West to settlement.

vation during the frigid weather, and nursed him back to health. On other occasions, Indians attacked and left him for dead; powerful grizzly bears lumbered through the forests toward him; branches from trees and branches lashed his face; rapids and streams tried to carry him away; bitter winters threatened to kill him. The sturdy mountain man endured each hazard.

In 1825 Beckwourth traveled to Yellowstone country. The Blackfeet Indians offered any willing group the chance to set up a fur trading post in their lands, but few takers came forward because most trappers refused to trust the fierce warriors. Though Beckwourth described the Blackfeet as "a tribe who prize white scalps very highly," he and another mountain man accepted their offer. In three weeks, Beckwourth had traded with the Blackfeet for thirty-nine packs of beaver fur.

Though he profited this time, he did not always live peacefully with the Blackfeet. Beckwourth was once traveling with a group of fur trappers and their families when a party of five hundred Blackfeet attacked. The men quickly gathered the women and children and pointed them toward a cluster of willow trees and shrubs about six miles distant. While their families hastened away, the men remained in the rear to slow down their adversaries.

Calling it "a running fight through the whole six miles," Beckwourth repeatedly risked his life. Beckwourth and a companion raced to rescue one man, but Blackfeet killed the trapper before they could get to him. Now almost surrounded, Beckwourth and his friend vaulted across a muddy depression and charged through a line of Blackfeet as "a shower of arrows and bullets whistled all around us."

Beckwourth's problems were far from over when he rejoined his companions in the willow patch. Though they now enjoyed some shelter, the trappers' meager ammunition supply would not long hold off the large numbers of Blackfeet. As Beckwourth later wrote, when the ammunition ran out, "what were we to do with an enemy more than ten times our number, who never grants or receives quarter?"

After a quick discussion, the trappers agreed they had little to lose in charging their foe. One trapper mentioned that they should "put our trust in God, and if we are to die, let us fall in protecting the defenseless. They will honor our memory for the bravery they witnessed."

Beckwourth and fifteen other screaming men charged out of the willows and broke through two groups of Blackfeet. In the swirl of battle, the Blackfeet shot Beckwourth's horse out from under him, then rushed forward to finish him off. An arrow creased the side of Beckwourth's head, but before the Blackfeet could move closer, another trapper rode up, Beckwourth jumped on behind him, and the two hustled back to the willows.

The only hope now lay in the slim chance that someone could ride out through the Blackfeet and get word to the main camp. "To risk a message there seemed to subject the messenger to inevitable death," Beckwourth recalled, "yet the risk must be encountered by some one." Beckwourth and a man named Calhoun volunteered for the dangerous mission and, after selecting the fastest horses, bolted out of the covering. Miraculously, they surprised their foe and broke through.

Before reaching the main camp, Beckwourth and Calhoun spotted a party of trappers and signaled that they needed help. One trapper raced back to his camp, while sixteen others rode forward. Beckwourth and Calhoun sped toward the willows with their reinforcements, rode though the surrounding Blackfeet, and rejoined a cheering group of trappers and their families. The Blackfeet, stunned by the arrival of Beckwourth's group, retreated when they saw the much larger band of trappers riding up from the main camp.

Though four trappers were killed and seven wounded, not one woman or child was injured during the fighting. Of the battle, Beckwourth recalled, "From the enemy we took seventeen scalps. The battle lasted five hours, and never in my whole life had I run such danger of losing my life and scalp. I now began to deem myself Indian-proof, and to think I never should be killed by them."

In fact, he developed strong ties with several Native American tribes, particularly the Crow Indians. In 1828 he and another trapper rode into a Crow village, hoping to obtain furs. An elderly woman who had long mourned the disappearance of her son stared at Beckwourth, then happily told the assembled villagers that this mountain man was her missing son. Beckwourth realized that if he went along with the misidentification, he most likely could have all the fur pelts he wanted, so he opted to remain with the Crows.

"I said to myself," he wrote later in his autobiography, "I can trap in their streams unmolested, and derive more profit under their protection than if among my own men, exposed incessantly to assassination and alarm."

For at least six years he blended in with the tribe, adopting their ways, marrying one of their women, and fighting their battles. He exhibited so much courage during the frequent clashes with neighboring tribes that the Crow named him Bloody Arm, chose him as a chief, and gave him a status he would never know in the white world. Beckwourth, now in his thirties, had at last found acceptance in a community.

However, enriched with furs and swayed by the independent spirit which dominated mountain men, Beckwourth departed sometime in the mid-1830s to embark upon a string of new adventures. From 1837-1838 he served as an Army scout in the Second Seminole War in Florida, then again turned west to set up trading posts in New Mexico and Colorado. When war flared up between the United States and Mexico, he rode as a dispatch rider for American units in California. After gold was discovered in California in 1849, Beckwourth joined the horde of prospectors flooding the region and set up a trading post in the Sierra Nevada Mountains, where he located a new path—Beckwourth Pass—leading down to the California coast.

After brief stints in Missouri and Colorado, Beckwourth shared his adventures with a writer named Thomas D. Bonner, who compiled the stories into a book. Titled *The Life and Adventures of James P. Beckwourth, Mountaineer, Scout, Pioneer, and Chief of the Crow Nation*, the book first appeared in 1856. Though the autobiography gave Beckwourth a bit of acclaim, he received not one penny for the effort. Bonner headed east with the material and was never heard from again.

The final years of Beckwourth's life brought controversy, sorrow, and regret to the aging mountain man. In 1864 Colonel J. M. Chivington of the Colorado Volunteers asked Beckwourth to scout for him during a campaign

One of the most renowned African Americans in the West, Beckwourth told of his adventures in his autobiography. The book brought him fame but little money.

against the Cheyenne. However, Beckwourth had no desire to fight. The weary man hoped to avoid the rigors of another campaign, and here he was facing an awkward situation: a white officer asking a black scout to help him locate and wipe out a Native American tribe—when for most of Beckwourth's life he had been treated far better by the continent's native inhabitants than by whites. Chivington gave him little choice, however, threatening to hang Beckwourth if he refused the request.

On November 28, 1864, Beckwourth guided a 750-man force to a Cheyenne village on the Sand Creek in the Colorado Territory. As dawn broke, Chivington opened his attack with the orders to "kill and scalp all Indians." Two chiefs that Beckwourth knew—White Antelope and Left Hand—walked toward the cavalry in an attempt to show that the villagers wanted peace, but soldiers gunned them down. Beckwourth watched in horror as White Antelope tried to stop the slaughter, "holding up his hands and saying, 'Stop! Stop!' He spoke it in as plain English as I can. He stopped and folded his arms until shot down."

Few Cheyenne escaped the massacre, as bloodthirsty cavalrymen and their fanatic colonel cut down and scalped six hundred men, women, and children. One soldier dragged a five-year-old girl from her hiding place and shot her through the head, and a stunned Beckwourth witnessed soldiers even scalping infants.

Beckwourth, remorseful over his role in the tragedy, later attempted to locate Cheyenne survivors of the Sand Creek Massacre. When he did, a Cheyenne friend of his, Leg-in-the-Water, bitterly asked, "What have you come here for; have you fetched the white man to finish killing our families again?"

Beckwourth answered that he hoped to arrange a truce, but the Cheyenne wanted none of that. One chief said, "The white man has taken our country, killed all our game; was not satisfied with that but killed our wives and children. Now no peace. We loved the whites until we found out they lied to us, and robbed us of what we had."

Beckwourth died in 1866. Ironically, he was again scouting for an army force on the move—this time against his beloved Crow Indians. He and another soldier rode alone into the Crow village, but only the soldier returned. According to the trooper, Beckwourth died in the chief's lodge.

One legend states that the Crows poisoned Beckwourth so that his potent spirit would forever remain with the tribe. If so, Beckwourth died among people who respected him for who he was—an appropriate ending for a memorable individual.

"Every Friend for Each Other"

Of all the occupations blacks held in the West, working as a cowboy offered the greatest amount of fairness. Blacks endured the same rigors, roped the same cattle, and received the same pay as white or Mexican cowboys. A man was judged more by how he performed, not how he looked. Though the almost 10,000 black cowboys who worked in the southwestern United States between 1870-1885 never achieved complete equality with their white counterparts, they lived far better lives than blacks who chose to remain in the South.

Bose Ikard's story illustrates this. Born a slave in Mississippi in 1847, Ikard moved to Texas with his master in 1852, where he quick-

Nicknamed Deadwood Dick because he won every event in a Deadwood, South Dakota rodeo, Nat Love could do it all—ride, rope, and shoot.

ly showed a talent for riding and roping. Freed at the end of the Civil War, he signed on at a ranch owned by one of the cattle industry's pioneers, Charles Goodnight.

Goodnight, who along with Oliver Loving carved out the Goodnight-Loving Trail through Texas for moving cattle to Denver and other railroad centers, warmed to Ikard's obvious skills with a horse and rope, but he was more impressed with the man's inner qualities. Ikard's sense of responsibility and his willingness to work hard led to a deep bond of trust between the cattle baron and former slave, and before long the two were almost inseparable.

If Goodnight carried a huge amount of money with him on the trail, he usually handed it to Ikard for safekeeping. Not only did Goodnight trust him, but he believed that thieves would never think of checking a black man's bedroll for cash. According to Goodnight, Ikard "surpassed any man I had in endurance and stamina. There was a dignity, a cleanliness, and a reliability about him that was wonderful. His behavior was very good in a fight, and he was probably the most devoted man to me that I ever had. I have trusted him farther than any living man. He was my detective, banker, and everything else in Colorado, New Mexico, and the other wild country I was in."

They faced numerous dangers together. Goodnight claimed that several times on the trail Ikard saved his life from Indians or outlaws. During one Indian attack, Ikard nursed the seriously wounded Goodnight while overseeing the rest of the men and the cattle.

Shortly before dawn one morning in 1867, Ikard sat on his horse, watching the herd while the other cowboys slept. Suddenly, the most

frightening sound a cowboy could hear rose out of the darkness—the rumblings of a stampede. Ikard spurred his horse and dashed along the herd's side in an attempt to get to the front, a dangerous move in light of the long, sharp horns wielded by the steer and the frequent prairie dog holes that could trip a horse and rider.

Of the sleeping men, Goodnight awoke first and ran in front of the camp, waving a blanket and yelling to divert the herd around his men. He then leaped onto his horse and rode out to slow the cattle. When Ikard spotted his boss behind the herd, he slowly started to swing the herd's leaders toward Goodnight, the proven manner of stopping a stampede.

When Goodnight caught up with Ikard, he wondered why his trusted rider had not tried to

Cowboys prepare to brand cattle on the western Plains. In the second half of the 19th century, African Americans found opportunities to work alongside whites in the West, driving cattle from ranches to railroad centers.

turn the herd sooner. Ikard replied that in the waning darkness he could not be sure who might be at the herd's rear, and he was afraid that Indians might have started the stampede. As soon as dawn's light permitted him a clear view of Goodnight, Ikard proceeded to turn the herd in upon itself.

The two men continued their close friendship until Ikard's death in 1929. Afterward, Goodnight erected a stone marker on his land in Ikard's memory which stated, "Served with me four years on the Goodnight-Loving Trail, never shirked a duty or disobeyed an order, rode with me in many stampedes, participated in three engagements with Comanches, splendid behavior."

Bose Ikard was honored in another manner when the writer of the popular book *Lonesome Dove* based one of his main characters on Ikard's life. Millions of viewers who tuned in to the story when it appeared as a television mini-series were thus exposed—many for the first time—to the contributions of blacks on the frontier.

Nat Love was another African American who gained notoriety as a cowboy, although in a much different fashion than Bose Ikard. His actual date of birth is unknown, for as Love later wrote, "no count was kept of such trivial matters as the birth of a slave baby." But sufficient records exist to show that he was born sometime in June 1854 in Davidson County, Tennessee, to one of the region's largest slave owners. Love's father died shortly after the Civil War ended, which placed all the responsibility for watching the family on Nat's twelve-year-old shoulders.

One way he helped support the family was by breaking wild horses for a neighbor. From this, Love developed a passion for the cowboy life, and he avidly listened to every yarn about cattle drives and immense Texas ranches spun by the men with whom he worked. He decided that his future lay to the west.

When it seemed in three to four years that he had brought stability to the family, Love set out on his journey west. Once in a while a friendly traveler offered Love a ride in his wagon, but usually he progressed on foot. When he finally arrived in Dodge City, Kansas, around 1869, Love wasted little time and approached the first trail boss he found. Fortunately, he located a Texas outfit that needed experienced cowboys.

The boss tested Love before giving him a job. "Can you ride?" he asked Love.

"Yes, sir," he replied.

Turning to another worker, the boss muttered, "Go out and rope old Good Eye," a horse known for his mean streak. Love jumped onto the peppy steed, which tried every trick it knew to throw the rider, but Love held on until Good Eye calmed down. The boss hired Love on the spot and told him to grab a horse, saddle, bridle, revolver, and other items he would need for the trail—words that must have made the former slave's head spin in delight.

Love worked on a ranch located along the Palo Duro River in the Panhandle for three years, driving cattle to Dodge City every spring and summer. Despite the trail's rigors, the life of a cowboy captivated Love, who soon became so skilled in roping and riding that, during a July 4, 1876, rodeo in Deadwood, South Dakota, he won every event on the program. From then on, other cowboys called him Deadwood Dick as a sign of respect.

Nat Love was one of the few black cowboys to receive any notice. Most, like these men in Texas, worked long hours and vanished, leaving behind nothing but their labors and sweat.

Though fame came his way, hazards swirled about him in equal proportion. In October 1876, as Love searched for strays, a band of Indians appeared. He tried to outride his pursuers, but they shot out his horse out from underneath him. Using the dead animal as protection, Love fought back until he fainted from the loss of blood caused by two wounds.

The captors carried Love to their camp and nursed him back to health. Though Love assumed they spared him because the tribe had "a large percentage of colored blood" and because they admired his bravery, as soon as a chance arrived Love crept out of his tepee under cover of darkness, jumped on a fast horse, and rode out.

Another story Love frequently shared, and included in his autobiography, was the ferocious

storm which almost killed him. His scared horse bolted and tossed him to the ground as it scampered away. Stranded on the Texas range with only a rifle, Love wandered around until he located a stray calf, which he killed for nourishment. As temperatures plunged to dangerous levels, Love huddled inside the split carcass for warmth and barely survived a frigid night. When morning dawned, little feeling remained in his nearly frozen hands, feet, and nose, and the cowboy looked more dead than alive when friends finally located him. Love lost the skin around his nose and mouth, plus the nails on his hands and feet. "I will never forget those few days when I was lost," Love recalled, "and the marks of that storm I will carry with me always."

In 1907 Love wrote his autobiography, called

The Life and Adventures of Nat Love, in which he recounted his exploits. Though many readers doubt the truth of his tales, for Love had a tendency to exaggerate, the book gives a unique glimpse into the life of a black cowboy. In it he stated that he never regretted one day of his work because Love knew that if he performed his job well, he would earn the respect of the other cowboys. On the trail, color often meant much less to men who needed a reliable hand.

When civilization advanced westward and drastically reduced the cowboy's domain, Love accepted a porter's job with one of the railroads that helped end the Wild West. Though Love had changed occupations, the cowboy in Love could never be extinguished. As he wrote, he reveled in everything the West offered, including

> the buffalo and other game, the Indians, the delight of living outdoors and the fights against death that caused every nerve to tingle, and the everyday communion with men whose minds were as broad as the plains they roamed and whose creed was every man for himself and every friend for each other and with each other till the end."

Though Barney Ford, another African American active in the West, never roped a steer, he developed businesses that catered to ranchers, cowboys, and other western profit-seekers. Barney Ford escaped from slavery before the Civil War started and made his way to Chicago, Illinois. When news arrived of the 1849 California gold strike, Ford decided he could make a handsome profit by starting a lodging house for prospectors. An ocean steamer transported Ford down the Atlantic coast to Central America, where an arduous excursion across Nicaragua to the Pacific coast awaited the passengers. Once across the narrow strip of land, travelers would then board another steamer for the voyage to California.

As Ford inched across Nicaragua with his group, he noticed the exhausted looks that pained each traveler. Already worn out from the bumpy Atlantic ride, plagued by the heat and bugs of Nicaragua, and yet to face another ocean transit, passengers longed for relief. Always prepared to seize any opportunity, Ford remained in Nicaragua and opened a hotel that offered fine food and rest to the flood of Americans who were sure to follow.

Ford amassed a handsome fortune before returning to Chicago, but he was far from finished. Learning of another gold strike, this time in Colorado, Ford tried to purchase a ticket on a stagecoach but was refused because of his color. Never one to let an obstacle stop him, Ford located a wagon train heading west and signed on as barber.

After succeeding in the mines, Ford opened a string of luxurious hotels in Denver and Cheyenne, particularly the three-story Inter-Ocean Hotel in Cheyenne, which was described by travelers as "one of the finest in the far West." Decorated with elegant carvings and ornate stairways, the hotel offered a taste of the East in the western lands.

In both Cheyenne and Denver, Ford's clever business talent earned the praise and respect of townspeople. He worked to improve racial relations and helped establish adult classes in reading and writing. Like Ikard and Love, Ford's work made an impact, not just on the communities in which he lived but on the people who followed.

"THE GREATEST SWEAT-AND-DIRT COWHAND"

N ot every black cowboy built his reputa- tion on the trail. Some took their skills to the rodeo, while one unearthed a bone which changed archaeologists' views of the arrival of humans on North America.

Bill Pickett may have been the most unique rodeo cowboy ever. Born sometime in the 1860s north of Austin, Texas, Pickett grew up around cowboys and animals. One day he watched a dog, trained to control cattle, lead a stray calf back to the herd by biting the animal's lip. The startled cow silently followed the dog back. Pick- ett wondered if that technique would work for him, so he grabbed a different calf and bit it on the lip. To his amazement, the calf stood still, allowing Pickett to toss it to the ground. He

A cowboy tries to stay in the saddle on a bucking bronco. Whether on the trail or in the rodeo, all cow- boys, black and white, had to be excellent riders.

Unique among cowboys, Bill Pickett wrestled steers to the ground by biting their lips.

practiced the strange style until he felt skilled enough to use it at county fairs.

Gradually, his fame spread around the Southwest. Though Pickett is given credit for originating the rodeo sport called bulldogging, in which a cowboy wrestles a steer to the ground, few other cowboys imitated his unique style. Pickett rode alongside the steer, jumped off a horse onto the steer's head, and grabbed a horn with each hand. He then twisted the horns until the steer's nose pointed up, when he reached under and clenched the steer's upper lip with his teeth. Flinging his hands to the side to show the audience that he only held the steer with his teeth, Pickett then fell to one side and dragged the steer until it dropped.

In the 1890s Pickett and his brothers formed the Pickett Brothers Bronco Busters and Rough Riders Association. Behind an ad which boldly declared, "We ride and break all wild horses with much care. Catching and taming wild cattle a specialty," the Picketts appeared in rodeos throughout the West, mainly in Texas and Arizona.

Doubtful spectators flooded to see Pickett. One man who attended a performance stated that "there were many in the audience who thought it would be impossible for a man to throw a steer with his teeth and the interest became intense" as Pickett appeared. As the cowboy neared his quarry, the crowd hushed in anticipation, then gasped as he leapt upon the steer's back, wrapped his arms around the steer's neck, and sank his teeth into its upper lip. Rapidly jerking back and forth, Pickett "forced the steer to its knees, then it rolled over on its side. The immense crowd cheered, and he again jumped on the back of the steer, which regained its feet, and repeated the performance."

His fame attracted the attention of the owners of the vast 101 Ranch in Oklahoma, who organized one of the most spectacular rodeos of the day. Containing every type of cowboy act, the 101 Wild West Show included cowboy Tom Mix, who later starred in films, and cowboy entertainer Will Rogers, who eventually became the nation's most popular public figure. Signing him in 1905, the promoters billed Pickett as "The Wonderful Negro 'Pickett', Throwing Wild Steer by the Nose with His Teeth," and toured the act throughout the United States, Canada, Mexico, and Europe.

The show's main organizer, Zach Miller of the 101 Ranch, had seen the best cowboys work on the range and perform in rodeos, and he bluntly stated, "Bill Pickett was the greatest sweat-and-dirt cowhand that ever lived—bar none." His feats in various shows confirmed that opinion. Before an enthusiastic crowd one night in New York's Madison Square Garden, a steer, frightened by the noise, darted out of the chute, crossed the arena, and barreled over the boards into the stands. As panicked spectators lunged out of the steer's way, Pickett charged up on his horse, jumped into the stands, and wrestled the runaway to the ground with his singular style. This amazing accomplishment, in which Pickett probably saved lives, garnered rave newspaper notices and ensured a successful run for the rodeo.

A 1908 show in Mexico City did not go as well, mainly because of advertising that unintentionally offended Mexico's citizens. After Miller claimed in ads that "Bill Pickett's bulldogging act was a greater show than any Mexican bull-fight," irate spectators poured into the arena. Stirred up by the insult to their national sport, the people booed and jeered all night.

Trying to calm matters, Zach Miller offered to donate $1,000 to charity if any Mexican bullfighter could duplicate Pickett's act. Mexico City's bullfighters countered with their own offer—they would wager 5,000 pesos that Pickett could not hold on to one of their fighting bulls for five minutes.

Pickett agreed to the arrangement and, before a boisterous crowd that hoped to witness a bloody goring by the bull, he faced his new foe. The bull slashed Pickett's horse with his horns as the cowboy drew close, but Pickett quickly grabbed the bull's tail, pulled himself up onto its back, then seized the bull's horns. The bull jerked Pickett from side to side and slammed him against the walls in furious attempts to shake its rider, but Pickett held on. When the bull slowed his movements, the Mexican spectators started throwing objects at Pickett, who almost lost his grip when a beer bottle smacked into his ribs.

Six minutes passed, but still Pickett held on. By now a bell should have signaled the event's end, but the Mexican worker controlling the bell refused to ring it. As angry shouts echoed throughout the arena, some of Pickett's fellow performers rode into the ring, roped the bull, and permitted Pickett to slide off. The crowd became so hostile that Mexican soldiers had to enter the arena and whisk the Americans to safety.

Though Pickett retired from the rodeo in the 1920s, he continued to give exhibitions. In 1923 he starred in a silent movie called "The Bull-Dogger" and followed that with appearances in a few more films.

Pickett suffered a huge loss in 1929 with the

death of Maggie, his wife of forty years with whom he had nine children. Three years later the only other man left from his rodeo days, Zach Miller, fell seriously ill. To cheer up his friend, Pickett performed his bulldogging act one more time, but the steer proved too quick for the aging Pickett and kicked him in the head. Eleven days later, on April 2, 1932, Pickett died from his injuries.

In recognition of Pickett's contributions to rodeo, in 1971 the cowboy movie star Joel McCrea inducted Pickett into the National Rodeo Cowboy Hall of Fame. Fittingly, Pickett was the first black cowboy to be included in the esteemed group.

Bill Pickett (front row, center with white shirt and dark bandana) poses in 1911 with other members of the successful 101 Wild West Show.

George McJunkin's fossil discovery proved that humans roamed the West thousands of years ago.

Another black cowboy achieved fame while out on the range, but his notoriety rested upon the discovery of something that, other than its location, had no connection to the West. Born a slave in Texas, George McJunkin headed to New Mexico when freed in 1865, where he worked on ranches as a horse breaker and trail driver.

One day in the mid-1920s, McJunkin was tracking down stray cattle along the edge of

Dead Horse Gulch when he spotted bones protruding from the gulch's side about twenty feet below the surface. Upon closer look, he noticed a solid object imbedded in the bones, which he pried out with his knife. It turned out to be a flint spearhead that looked much different from the arrowheads he usually found in the region.

Eventually, word of McJunkin's find reached Dr. J. D. Figgins, a Colorado paleontologist. Intrigued, he traveled to the scene and uncovered the bones of ancient bison and several more flint spearheads. Though no human bones were found, the discovery was named Folsom Man because it rested near the town of Folsom, and Figgins knew that a human being had to have shaped the flint weapons. Scientific tests made on the bison bones dated the remains as at least 10,000 years old, proving that humans were living in southwestern North America by approximately 8,000-10,000 B. C.

McJunkin may not have wrestled hardened steers to the ground or battled outlaws, but the significance of his discovery will remain long after the memory of most other cowboys has disappeared.

"A Most Ferocious Monster"

Ned Huddleston, alias Isom Dart, alias the Black Fox, alias the Calico Cowboy, straddled both sides of the law in his action-packed career. Born a slave in Arkansas in 1849, Huddleston was freed when the Civil War ended. The 16-year-old drifted south to Mexico, where he worked for a time as a stunt rider and clown in a circus before teaming with an outlaw named Terresa. The two stole horses, swam them across the Rio Grande River into Texas, and sold them to American ranchers.

Since this occupation normally guaranteed that an angry group of Mexican ranchers would be continuously trying to track him down and kill him, Huddleston soon departed for the Southwest. His love of horses and natural touch with the animals made him a valuable member

Though leading a life of crime, Ned Huddleston also exhibited decency and a warm sense of humor. Unfortunately for him, his outlaw ways cost him his life in 1900.

of a ruthless group of horse thieves. Known as the Gault Gang, the rustlers operated out of infamous Brown's Hole, a hiding spot in northwest Colorado populated by notorious outlaws, including Robert Leroy Parker, better known to history as Butch Cassidy.

As in Mexico, if one makes a living stealing horses, one better be good—or lucky—at dodging angry ranchers and their bullets. Huddleston was both. One collection of horse ranchers hoped to set an ambush for the Gault Gang at one of the gang's hiding spots. On the way back to camp a horse kicked and critically injured Joe Pease, one of the outlaws, so Huddleston volunteered to remain with his dying friend. The rest of the gang rode ahead.

Huddleston remained with the dying Pease for almost two days. When Pease passed away, Huddleston returned to camp—again empty as the others were out rustling horses—to get a shovel for burial. While Huddleston headed back to dig a grave for Pease, the ranchers located and surrounded the vacant camp, then waited for their revenge. Before long Gault and the others trotted in and dismounted. Suddenly, a flurry of gunshots rang out from all directions, and in minutes every member of the gang lay dead.

Huddleston, one half mile away with Pease, heard the gunshots and guessed what was occurring, so he stayed where he was and hoped the ranchers would overlook him. Through a long night Huddleston, happy to be alive but most likely uncomfortable with his nighttime accommodations, hid in the open grave with Pease's body.

The next morning Huddleston cautiously emerged from the grave and approached the camp, where he found the dead bodies of his comrades. After removing their money belts, Huddleston hurried away.

Huddleston rode to Oklahoma, where he changed his name to Isom Dart, briefly abandoned his life of crime, and raised cotton. Before long, though, he had joined another gang of rustlers operating out of Brown's Hole.

This time a determined lawman halted Huddleston's activities. Deputy Sheriff Joseph Philbrick of Wyoming, spurred on by a generous reward offered by Wyoming ranchers, rode right in to Brown's Hole and arrested a surprised Huddleston. Returning with his prisoner along the trail to Wyoming, Philbrick's horses bolted, threw Philbrick hard onto the ground, and knocked down an incline the buckboard upon which they were riding. Rather than abandon the unconscious lawman, Huddleston nursed Philbrick's injuries, retrieved the horses, and righted the buckboard. Gently placing the sheriff into the wagon, Huddleston drove to Rock Springs, Wyoming, took Philbrick to a hospital, and surrendered at the local jail.

The residents of Rock Springs treated Huddleston like a hero for helping their lawman, and when he stood trial for stealing horses, Philbrick appeared in his behalf as a character witness. The jury wasted little time finding Huddleston not guilty, figuring that any man who acted as Huddleston did posed no threat to their community.

Huddleston returned to Brown's Hole, probably feeling he had more lives than a cat. Though still associating with outlaws, he developed a tamer side by forming a close association with the McKnights, a family in the area with two children. Huddleston often visited the couple's home, where he loved relating stories of his slave days and his subsequent escapades and kept the children laughing with a steady stream of jokes. One of the youngsters exclaimed delightedly to their mother, "Mamma, I'll never have to go to the circus, 'cause I got a circus all my own."

Huddleston, a curious mixture of good and evil, now decided to settle down and earn a living by breaking horses. Eventually, he saved enough money to purchase his own horse ranch and formed a partnership with another former rustler, Matt Rash. Cowboys working on the ranch continued to be impressed with Huddleston's skills. One stated that, "I have seen all the great riders, but for all-around skill as a cowman, Isom Dart was unexcelled and I never saw his peer."

Unfortunately for Huddleston, his criminal past was about to catch up to him. Wyoming cattlemen, still determined to get revenge on the rustlers, hired the infamous murderer-detective, Tom Horn, to track down Rash and Huddleston. The hired killer rode into Brown's Hole and shadowed the two men. Finally, as Rash ate breakfast on July 10, 1900, Horn crawled within rifle range and mortally shot the outlaw.

The fifty-year-old Dart refused to run from the bounty hunter, stating that he was too old to hide out and that he preferred to work on his farm. Horn, who would have tracked down Huddleston no matter where he fled, cautiously stalked his man until he had a certain shot. In early October 1900, as Huddleston stepped out the front door of his cabin, Horn executed the thief with an accurate blast from 196 yards.

Crawford Goldsby, born near Fort Concho, Texas, on February 8, 1876, shared none of the compassion or decency that Huddleston could summon on occasion. Instead, murder and violence followed in his wake.

His father, George Goldsby, served as a trooper in the Tenth Cavalry, a unit known throughout the West as the Buffalo Soldiers. Goldsby's mother, Ellen Beck, was a black who bore one-quarter Cherokee blood.

Though their son briefly attended the highly-regarded Indian Industrial School at Carlisle, Pennsylvania, from which heralded athlete Jim Thorpe emerged, he quickly dropped out and started a sordid life of crime. While in his early teens, Goldsby argued with another black youth named Jake Lewis near Fort Gibson, Indian Territory, shot him twice, then fled to avoid arrest. He joined a gang of train robbers called the Cook Gang, where he took the name Cherokee Bill.

Bill's inclination toward violence made his compatriots look tame by comparison. During one train holdup, Bill brutally gunned down a station agent. He murdered his own brother-in-law, George Brown, supposedly because Brown's father had given Brown and his wife more hogs than he gave Bill. After killing Brown, Cherokee Bill hovered over the lifeless corpse and, with a savagery that shocked even those accustomed to seeing violence on the frontier, riddled Brown's body with bullets.

Western communities so feared the man that one town council, hoping to protect its peaceable citizens, passed a law forbidding anyone from laying a hand on Cherokee Bill whenever he rode in. No one knows for sure how many people he murdered—some claim as high as thirty-six— but the teenage killer spread enough bloodshed across the land that by his nineteenth birthday, a hefty reward had been placed on his head. Few

Crawford Goldsby, alias Cherokee Bill, left a trail of blood and violence in his wake. He was arrested and hanged before his 21st birthday.

men jumped at the chance to collect the cash, however, since Cherokee Bill's skill with a weapon and volatile temper made him "the most feared desperado in the Indian Territory."

Finally a bold law officer, Deputy W. C. Smith, snared the wanted man with the help of an acquaintance, Ike Rogers, who was friendly with Cherokee Bill. The two used one of Bill's girl-friends, Maggie Glass, as bait. Rogers invited Glass to his home, then got word to Bill that Glass wanted to see him. When the outlaw rode in, Rogers and a man named Clint Scales chatted with Bill in the hopes of getting him to relax his guard. This stretched through the evening and on into the next morning, however, as Chero-kee Bill refused to let go of his Winchester rifle, even in the company of his supposed friends.

Rogers and Scales spotted their chance early the next morning. As Bill bent over the fire-place to light a cigarette, Rogers crept up behind him and cracked him over the head with a stick of firewood. Rogers later related how "I must have hit him hard enough to kill an ordinary man, but it only knocked him down. Scales and I jumped on him but he let out a yell and got on his feet."

After a prolonged struggle, the two managed to silence the dazed criminal and put handcuffs on him. Ignoring Bill's shouts to either kill him or let him go, they placed him on a wagon and, with Scales driving and Rogers following at a safe distance behind with a double-barreled shot-gun leveled at their prisoner, they transported him to Fort Smith to stand trial for murder.

The heavily-guarded thug had little hope for freedom, especially since he appeared in Judge Charles Parker's court. Labeled the "Hanging Judge" for his willingness to speedily dispense

Ike Rogers (far right) and Clint Scales (second right) stand with their prisoner, (center) following Cherokee Bill's arrest.

justice with a rope, Parker took no pains to hide his repulsion for Cherokee Bill. When the lawyers finished arguing, Parker delivered such a harsh image of the defendant in his instructions that it took the jury only minutes to find Cherokee Bill guilty. Following the verdict's announcement, Bill's mother broke down in tears, but the condemned man briefly glanced at her and mumbled, "What's the matter with you? I'm not a dead man yet by a long ways."

He almost made good on his word. Someone smuggled in two guns to Bill, apparently by attaching them to a long pole and sticking them through a window in the cell's rear. Bill put one gun in a bucket, intending that it be found, and concealed the other, with extra ammunition, behind a brick in the wall. Who, he reasoned, would expect a second gun to be in the cell after discovering the first?

On July 26, 1895, two prison guards, Camp-

One of the lawmen who worked for Judge Parker was African American. In this photograph, four marshals, two of them black, rest while tracking criminals.

bell Eoff and Lawrence Keating, started their nightly check of prisoners. When Keating came to Bill's cell, the prisoner pointed his pistol at him through the bars and told him to hand over his weapon. The surprised guard tried to draw his gun, but Bill shot him before he got the chance. Eoff ran down the hall and barely escaped a flurry of Bill's bullets.

As shots rang down the hallway and transformed the narrow passage into a smoke-filled path, Bill barricaded himself in his cell and fought it out. The situation looked bleak until another prisoner sentenced to be hanged for murder, Henry Starr, offered a deal to the deputy marshal. "If you'll keep the men who are watching the corridor from shooting at me, I'll go into Cherokee Bill's cell and get his gun for you."

The lawman agreed and ordered his men to stop firing. Starr carefully edged toward Bill, disappeared into the cell, and emerged a few minutes later with Bill's gun. No one learned how Starr convinced the condemned man to surrender, but influential people arranged to have Starr's conviction changed to manslaughter as a reward. Within five years Starr was a free man.

Cherokee Bill stood trial for the Keating murder, and not surprisingly a second jury delivered a guilty verdict faster than the first. A delighted Parker ordered assistants to "give these men a good dinner. They deserve it," then turned his wrath on the criminal. "You are undoubtedly the most ferocious monster, and your record more atrocious than all the criminals who have hitherto stood before this bar."

An enormous throng gathered around the prison and rushed to rooftops to get a glimpse of Cherokee Bill on March 17, 1896—execution day for the twenty-year-old killer. When Bill emerged from prison and noticed the crowd, he muttered to his guard, "Look at the people; something must be going to happen."

Before a guard placed the hood over Bill's head, he asked if the outlaw had any last words. "No," Bill responded. "I came here to die—not to make a speech."

After a minister said a final prayer, a guard placed the noose about Cherokee Bill's neck. Eoff, given the task of springing the trap door, asked Bill to move over so that he stood directly on the door. In possibly the only time that Cherokee Bill ever obeyed a lawman, he shuffled over a few feet, then plunged to his death.

"I Never Witnessed Better Courage"

Any history of the West finds room for the exploits of the United States Army, especially the cavalry. That is as it should be, for the stirring deeds performed by soldiers on and off horseback have long fascinated book lovers and moviegoers. For a long time only one side of the story reached the public—that of the white soldier. In recent years, the tale has fortunately been broadened to include the Native American point of view. One injustice remains, however—the military contributions of African Americans in the westward movement.

Four distinguished units of black soldiers served in the various Western campaigns—the Ninth and Tenth Cavalry and the Twenty-fourth and Twenty-fifth Infantry Regiments. Raised

Native Americans like Sitting Bull received harsh treatment from whites similar to that experienced by African Americans. Ironically, in spite of this the two groups were frequent foes on Western battlefields.

African Americans, such as these members of the all-black Ninth Cavalry, served their nation by protecting settlers in the West.

by a July 28, 1866, act of Congress that offered $13 per month to each man, the units contained as many as 1,000 soldiers, who were commanded by white officers. The regiments filled quickly as many former slaves enlisted, drawn by the money, a chance to improve their lives, and prospect for adventure. One enlistee explained, "I got tired of looking mules in the face from sunrise to sunset. Thought there must be a better livin' in this world."

As a sign of recognition for their foes' courage, Native Americans dubbed these men Buffalo Soldiers because the curly hair of some resembled that of the revered buffalo, and because in winter the soldiers wore buffalo skins for warmth. Their tasks varied, but generally they did what other military men did—protected settlers, escorted stagecoaches and survey parties through dangerous lands, and prevented Indian raids. The black soldier found himself in a unique situation in the West—he fled discrimination by the whites back East, only to risk his own life protecting other whites from being killed by yet a third group, Native Americans, whose rights were being trampled on by white settlers.

Though the black soldiers received harsh treatment from their white officers and frequently had to make do with inferior equipment and rotten food, they performed admirably, receiving for bravery eighteen Medals of Honor, the nation's highest military honor. Sergeant Emanuel Stance earned the first medal on May 20-21, 1870, near Kickapoo Springs, Texas. Searching for two kidnapped white children, Stance and the nine men he led spotted a group of warriors preparing to attack a wagon train. To forestall the attack, he led a charge that scattered the Indians, in spite of "bullets whistling about their ears." Stance continued searching for the children and eventually freed them from their captors the next day.

When he was awarded the Medal of Honor, Stance proudly stated, "I will cherish the gift as a thing of priceless value and endeavor by my future conduct to merit the high honor conferred upon me."

Another sergeant, Brent Woods of the Ninth Cavalry, saved almost forty lives on August 19, 1881, during an expedition against the Apache chief Nana. Twenty-five soldiers, including Woods, and twenty cowboys led by their boss, rancher George Daly, rode into Apache land in southwestern New Mexico. When the force approached the opening to Gavilan Canyon, a perfect spot for an ambush, the white officer in charge ordered his men to wait for reinforcements before riding into the canyon. An impa-

Buffalo Soldiers accompany a stagecoach as it crosses the Great Plains.

tient Daly, however, led his cowboys through the pass, forcing the officer to advance his men into the canyon to protect the reckless rancher.

Once the entire group rode into the canyon's confines, Nana's warriors opened a withering fire that killed the white officer and Daly. Soldiers and cowboys alike, now leaderless, scrambled for cover and tried to control their panic.

Suddenly, Sergeant Brent Woods rose, gathered the soldiers together and, according to the official report, "led them in a charge against one side of the canyon, and fought his way desperately to a high piece of ground, driving the Indians before him." He then mounted a second charge against the canyon's other side that forced Nana and his survivors to flee into Mexico. One of the cowboys mentioned of the courageous Woods, "If it had not been for him none of us could have come out of that canyon."

Two men from the Twenty-fourth, Sergeant Benjamin Brown and Corporal Isaiah Mays, won the Medal of Honor during a May 11, 1889, action. They fought so valiantly to protect an army payroll wagon when it was attacked that the white paymaster, who had previously served in the Civil War as part of Ulysses S. Grant's regiment, concluded, "I never witnessed better courage or better fighting than shown by these colored soldiers on May 11, 1889."

This type of action, and others such as helping to track down Billy the Kid and Geronimo, earned the Buffalo Soldiers grudging respect and, in some cases, open admiration from the white settlers and ranchers they protected. When members of the Twenty-fifth Infantry Regiment prepared to leave Missoula, Montana, in the late 1890s to serve in the Spanish-American War, the town's citizens rescheduled Easter Sunday services so they could line up along Missoula's main street and give them a cheerful farewell.

One Buffalo Soldier deserves special mention for the racial barrier he shattered. Born into slavery on March 21, 1856, in Thomasville, Georgia, Henry O. Flipper moved to Atlanta with his family when his master relocated there. He learned to read and write from another slave, and after the Civil War he attended schools set up by the American Missionary Association. He performed so well that in 1869 he was admitted to the army's military academy at West Point to begin training as an officer.

He faced a bitter four years during which none of the other students would speak to him unless official business required it. While the teachers and other officers stationed at West Point treated him fairly in class, Flipper learned to keep his mouth closed and endure the isolation. It was hard, though. "There was no society for me to enjoy. No friends, male or female, for me to visit."

His isolation threatened to worsen when, in 1873, he became the first black graduate of West Point. Of the army's 2,100 officers, Flipper was the sole black. When he arrived at his first post with the Tenth Cavalry at Fort Sill, Indian Territory, white officers shunned him.

In 1880 Flipper and the Tenth Cavalry were transferred to Fort Davis, Texas, to help stamp out a Mescalero Apache uprising led by a chief named Victorio. Flipper fought well in one action, where his unit sprinted in on their horses to rescue another group of soldiers trapped near Eagle Springs. As Flipper wrote in his journal, "We came in a swinging gallop for fifteen or twenty miles. We got right into it and soon had the Indians on the run."

Flipper was appointed the post quartermaster and commissary at Fort Davis. The man in this position held responsibility for housing, food acquisition, and supplies and thus controlled a significant amount of money—far from being a minor job. Many of the white officers resented that Flipper held the post, and their hatred skyrocketed when Flipper often accompanied a white girl on horseback rides.

Suddenly the commanding officer at Fort Davis, Colonel W. R. Shafter, charged Flipper with stealing money from the army. Flipper angrily denied the accusation and claimed that bigoted white officers wanted him removed from the fort. Even though he was acquitted of stealing, especially when a high-ranking officer came to his defense, Flipper was found guilty of "conduct unbecoming an officer" and forced to leave the army.

A bitter Flipper spent his remaining years

as a civil and mining engineer, first in Mexico and then in Washington, D. C., where a sympathetic politician, Senator Albert B. Fall, hired him as a consultant. After working with Fall for eleven years, Flipper finished his career as a consultant to Latin American oil companies before retiring in 1931.

Isaiah Dorman's name will not be found among the Buffalo Soldiers, but he served in the military and fought in one of the nation's most famous battles—Lt. Colonel George A. Custer's 1876 fight at the Little Bighorn.

Little is known of his life before the Civil War. Dorman supposedly escaped from slavery in either Louisiana or Alabama in the 1840s. On November 11, 1865, the War Department hired him as a messenger carrier, and for two years Dorman transported military messages one hundred miles between Western outposts in the Dakota Territory. After this, he disappeared into the wilderness and lived with the Sioux Indians, where he married a Sioux wife and befriended Chief Sitting Bull. In 1871 he again worked for the army, this time as a scout and guide for a railroad survey team. Following this duty he served as an interpreter.

Fate dealt Dorman an unlucky card when the army assigned him to Custer's Seventh Cavalry on May 14, 1876, a scant five weeks before Custer led his men to death. Since Dorman had lived with the Sioux and spoke their language, he was considered a valuable addition to Custer's unit.

On June 25, 1876, Custer's cavalry approached a Sioux village near the Little Bighorn River in Montana. Custer, itching for a fight, hastily divided his force into three battalions—

Captain Frederick W. Benteen was ordered to search the valley for Indians, while Major Marcus A. Reno led a charge across the river against the camp. Custer planned to attack with the third force against the village's side and rear.

Dorman rode against the village with Major Reno. Before they reached the intended target, throngs of warriors swooped down on Reno and his men and turned this arm of Custer's assault into a shambles. Reno ordered a speedy withdrawal which, because of the large numbers of Sioux and other warriors, could not be accomplished in an organized fashion. Each man was on his own, mostly with disastrous results.

Dorman did not get far before Sioux fighters, angered that a man who had lived among them had apparently turned traitor and led Custer against the Sioux, overwhelmed the scout. One chief recalled, "We passed a black man in a soldier's uniform and we had him. He turned on his horse and shot an Indian right through the heart. Then the Indians fired at this one man and riddled his horse with bullets."

Dorman struggled to get out from underneath his horse and return fire. Another soldier who survived the battle, Private Roman Rutten, saw Dorman as Rutten raced by on his horse. The horseless Dorman, down on one knee and firing at the Sioux, glanced at Rutten and shouted, "Good-bye, Rutten!"

Another soldier who hid in a willow thicket watched the scout die. "I saw Indians shooting at Isaiah and squaws pounding him with stone hammers. His legs below the knees were shot full of bullets."

Some accounts state that Dorman's old friend, Sitting Bull, walked over to the dying scout and offered him a drink of water before

Isaiah Dorman died in the battle along the Little Bighorn River when George Armstrong Custer, pictured, led his men in a futile assault.

he died. Most of the Sioux warriors, however, were pleased with Dorman's death.

The United States government erected a huge monument at the battlefield in 1881 which honored the slain soldiers. The first and last name of each officer and cavalryman was etched into the granite slab. That is, except for Isaiah Dorman. His first name is all that appears, a slight that practically wipes the memory of this black scout from the pages of Western history. Slain by the Sioux because he helped the white soldiers, Dorman was now forgotten by the same army which had employed him.

"His Bill Is Paid"

Black women comprised an important part of the story of African Americans in the West. Like the other characters who have been portrayed in this book, women possessed the same skills, braved similar dangers, and achieved success in equal measure.

Born in 1832, Mary Fields fled Tennessee slavery and settled in Ohio at an early age. She formed a close friendship with a nun at a local school and was heartbroken when the nun was transferred to Cascade, Montana. The two maintained a correspondence through the years, and when Fields learned in 1884 that her friend had fallen gravely ill, she abandoned Ohio to nurse the nun back to health.

Now fifty-two years old, Fields applied for a job transporting supplies through the harsh Montana terrain from Cascade to the nearby Catholic mission where her friend lived. The nuns loved working with Fields, who always delivered the supplies, even in the worst winter weather.

Female African Americans braved the same hazards as males and performed extraordinary feats.

Fields, six feet tall and weighing over two hundred pounds, was expert in using a rifle, pistol, and horses. Settlers learned not to anger Fields, who normally packed a small pistol, smoked cigars, and downed large amounts of whiskey. She feared no one around—man or woman—and the few men who challenged her to a fistfight quickly regretted their brashness.

One night, as Fields drove her supply wagon to the mission, a pack of wolves frightened the horses. The panicked animals bolted—which dumped the wagon on its side—and ran off, leaving Fields to face the wolves on foot. After building a fire from sagebrush, Fields kept the wolves away with her rifle and revolver until dawn. At first light she righted the wagon, reloaded the supplies, then pulled the wagon into town.

Fields's eight-year career hauling freight to the nuns ended abruptly. Another worker at the mission insulted Fields, who instantly challenged him to a duel. After his shot missed its mark, Fields carefully aimed and fired close enough to the man's head to frighten him. The local Catholic official in the area, Bishop Brondel, saw little humor in the incident, and fired Fields.

The nuns helped Fields open a restaurant in Cascade, which she operated with typical bluntness. On one occasion, as Fields stood at the bar of a local saloon—Cascade's mayor had given Fields permission to drink in the all-male establishments—chomping on a cigar and downing whiskey, she spotted a man enter who owed Fields for some laundry she had done.

"Hey, come here, you. When are you going to pay me for that laundry?"

The frightened customer sprinted out of the saloon, but Fields chased after, caught up to

him, and pinned him to the ground. "If you don't pay me the $2.00 you owe me for that laundry, you won't get up," she bellowed. After collecting her money, Fields returned to the saloon, stepped up to the bar, and announced, "His laundry bill is paid."

Mary's restaurant failed because she gave

away so many free meals to travelers who had no money. The nuns once again helped her, this time in a stagecoach business, in which she hauled passengers and freight through the Montana Territory. Though stagecoach drivers usually had to keep a wary eye out for bandits, few outlaws bothered the driver, labeled "Stagecoach Mary," because she so determinedly guarded her cargo.

Mary Fields died in 1914. In a sign of honor for one of Cascade's leading citizens, town officials closed the schools on that day.

Like Mary Fields, Biddy Mason was born a slave, but their lives took different paths. When her master, Robert Smith, moved to California in 1850, the thirty-eight-year-old Mason and her three daughters accompanied him.

Six years later, her master again wanted to relocate—this time to Texas—but Mason refused to go. Since California's government did not recognize slavery, she claimed that she and her daughters were free and asked a local court to decide the issue. A federal court in Los Angeles agreed and declared Mason and her family free in 1856.

After earning money as a nurse and a housekeeper, Mason invested her savings in land purchases. Her acquisitions were so successful that by the end of the 1880s, she was worth over $200,000, an incredible amount for those days. Along with her husband, Los Angeles businessman Charles P. Owens, she became the most prominent figure in the town's black community. The couple freely donated money to help poor blacks get on their feet, and they gave land for schools and churches.

Like Mary Fields, Biddy Mason earned the

respect of the community in which she lived. By the time she died in 1891, she had influenced the lives of hundreds of people in the Los Angeles area.

Mason and Fields were just two of the thousands of African-Americans who created new lives for themselves on the American frontier. Even before black men and women received the rights of full citizenship in the United States—this would not occur until the 1960s—their efforts as soldiers, cowboys, and settlers added significantly to the nation's westward development. The exploits and successes of these African-American pioneers opened the West to other settlers of all races and changed forever America's history.

CHRONOLOGY

April 26, 1798	James Beckwourth is born on a Virginia slave plantation
1823	James Beckwourth joins the Rocky Mountain Fur Company
1832	Mary Fields is born a slave in Tennessee
1837-1838	James Beckwourth scouts for the Army during the Second Seminole War
1847	Bose Ikard is born a slave in Mississippi
1849	Former slave Barney Ford opens a Nicaragua hotel
1849	James Beckwourth heads to California during the gold rush
1849	Ned Huddleston is born a slave in Arkansas
1850	Biddy Mason, a slave, moves to California with her master
June, 1854	Nat Love is born a slave in Tennessee
1856	*The Life and Adventures of James P. Beckwourth* is published
1856	A Los Angeles federal court declares Biddy Mason a free person
March 21, 1856	Henry O. Flipper is born a slave in Georgia
November 28, 1864	James Beckwourth guides Colonel J. M. Chivington's force to Sand Creek in the Colorado Territory
November 11, 1865	War Department hires Isaiah Dorman as a message carrier
1866	James Beckwourth dies
July 28, 1866	Congress passes an act forming four military units of black soldiers
1867	Bose Ikard helps stop a cattle stampede
1869	Nat Love arrives in Dodge City and joins a Texas cattle outfit
1869	Henry Flipper enters West Point
May 20-21, 1870	Sergeant Emanuel Stance earns a Medal of Honor for actions near Kickapoo Springs, Texas
1873	Henry Flipper becomes the first black to graduate from West Point
February 8, 1876	Crawford Goldsby, alias Cherokee Bill, is born in Texas

May 14, 1876	Isaiah Dorman is assigned to Custer's Seventh Cavalry
June 25, 1876	Isaiah Dorman dies during Custer's Last Stand
July 4, 1876	Nat Love wins every event in a Deadwood, South Dakota rodeo
October, 1876	Nat Love lives with an Indian tribe
1881	The United States government inscribes only Isaiah Dorman's first name on the Custer battlefield monument
August 19, 1881	Sergeant Brent Woods earns a Medal of Honor for his actions in Gavilan Canyon, New Mexico
1884	Mary Fields moves to Montana
May 11, 1889	Sergeant Benjamin Brown and Corporal Isaiah Mays earn Medals of Honor for protecting an army payroll wagon
1891	Biddy Mason dies in Los Angeles
July 26, 1895	Cherokee Bill kills a prison guard during an unsuccessful attempt to break out
March 17, 1896	Cherokee Bill is hanged
October, 1900	Tom Horn kills Ned Huddleston
1905	Bill Pickett joins the 101 Ranch's Wild West Show
1907	*The Life and Adventures of Nat Love* is published
1908	Bill Pickett rides a bull in Mexico City
1914	Mary Fields dies in Cascade, Montana
1923	Bill Pickett stars in "The Bull-Dogger," a silent film
1929	Bose Ikard dies
April 2, 1932	Bill Pickett dies
1971	Bill Pickett becomes the first black cowboy to be inducted into the National Rodeo Cowboy Hall of Fame

FURTHER READING

Anderson, LaVere. *Saddles and Sabres: Black Men in the Old West.* Champaign, Illinois: Garrard Publishing Company, 1975.

Cox, Clinton. *The Forgotten Heroes: The Story of the Buffalo Soldiers.* New York: Scholastic Inc., 1993.

Durham, Philip and Everett L. Jones. *The Negro Cowboys.* Lincoln, Nebraska: University of Nebraska Press, 1965.

Heard, J. Norman. *The Black Frontiersmen.* New York: The John Day Company, 1969.

Love, Nat. *The Life and Adventures of Nat Love.* Lincoln, Nebraska: University of Nebraska Press, 1995.

Pelz, Ruth. *Black Heroes of the Wild West.* Seattle, Washington: Open Hand Publishing Inc., 1990.

Schlissel, Lillian. *Black Frontiers: A History of African American Heroes in the Old West.* New York: Simon & Schuster Books for Young Readers, 1995.

Slatta, Richard W. *The Cowboy Encyclopedia.* New York: W. W. Norton & Company, 1994.

Stewart, Paul W. and Wallace Yvonne Ponce. *Black Cowboys.* Broomfield, Colorado: Phillips Publishing, Inc., 1986.

Wellman, Paul I. *A Dynasty of Western Outlaws.* New York: Bonanza Books, 1961.

INDEX

PICTURE CREDITS

ABOUT THE AUTHOR

John F. Wukovits is a teacher and writer from Trenton, Michigan who specializes in history and sports. His work has appeared in more than 25 national publications, including *Wild West* and *American History*. His books include a biography of the World War II commander Admiral Clifton Sprague, and he has written biographies of Barry Sanders, Jesse James, Wyatt Earp, and Vince Lombardi for Chelsea House. A graduate of the University of Notre Dame, Wukovits is the father of three daughters—Amy, Julie, and Karen.